©2020 D. Saige Elldurs
first printing June 2020

all rights reserved worldwide

This book of satire is dedicated to my old childhood friend Jiblet McFlangehandel

D. Saige Elldurs

Forward

Welcome to the brave new world of the dystopian dreamtime, the new age of reconciled improbabilities and alternative facts swinging in among the standard political doublespeak that comes from forked tongues wearing two faces.
But you know that even alternative facts can have alternatives, and that's why this book is for you!
Every fact doesn't have to be true and you accept that as a true fact.
Full of newly adapted stories for your personal accruement of knowledge, this book can be a base, a platform if you will, for you to launch your own peculiar view of the world and it's workings.
Truth, as we now know, having been told by our highest government leaders, is always malleable and is not always true. There are alternative facts, just like there are alternative realities, and alternative lifestyles.
It doesn't matter what the evidence proves; arguments over truth, like arguments in court, are not about finding truth itself, but rather it is about who can win the argument. You understand that it doesn't matter what others think, you now have here in your hands a book of facts and you are going to read them all!
So read, enjoy, and be sure to call your favorite radio host, or write to your favorite newspaper, and express your firm support for and belief in these fancy new truestuffs.
They might not be self evident, but this book certainly makes them clear.

Dr. Pauolo Genero, PhD & D. Saige Elldurs

Valencia Orange, California

2020

True Stories

During Americas colonial years while the bulk of the colonies was built of logs and mud the countries to the south, Mexico, Columbia, Argentina among others were very civilized, built of stone with universities and operas and a certain wild yet refined elegance.
That still pisses off Americans.

Australia was originally settled by male convicts and no women. After a few months the prisoners figured out that when a koala is tugged hard back against the tree its recurved claws stick deep in the tree trunk preventing the koala from moving away. This gave the convicts plenty of time to rape the koalas at their leisure.

Disgusted on finding a large number of koalas still stuck on tree trunks after having been recently raped to death the authorities passed legislation forbidding the rape of wildlife, and specifically koalas. Those laws are still on the books to this day in New South Wales.

The government also began importing prostitutes for the convicts carnal pleasures, but many of what would soon be known as 'Australians' later swore that there was "nothing quite like that fluffy sweet koala stuck in there 'round about waist high on an old gum tree....yeah."

"Cardinal Compass Points Be Damned!"

Moses spent 40 years wandering around aimlessly in a space roughly the size of Maricopa County in Arizona. At what point did his followers pull him aside and say, "hey Moses, just pick a direction and stick with it ok?" They didn't. That didn't happen because, cardinal compass points be damned, Moses was in charge and consequently his particular alternative facts were the only facts that mattered!*

*His followers were actually kind of scared shitless to confront him for fear he would try to destroy their livelihoods or reputations...no one wants to confront a madman who claims to talk to flaming shrubbery and animated mountaintop boulders, so their fears were fairly understandable...and for those saying compasses had not been invented yet I suggest that it doesn't take a genius to follow the sunset...

Neck tattoos were first introduced by Johann Soztig, an early barber and surgeon, as a cure for masturbation.
Curiously this has no bearing on the proven fact that people with neck tattoos are wankers.

There is only one invisible friend and that invisible friend is a friend to all
so there is no use in arguing about who's invisible friend is better because
ultimately they are all the same invisible friend.
Which is why only lesser sorts would argue over who has the better
invisible friend since everyone who is anyone knows that
the only real friend in this life is personal wealth,
vast tangible mine-not-yours hoards of glorious spendoolies.

In 1843 a patent was issued in England for a device "used for the introduction of voles and other small animals into the rectum". Basically just a tube with one closed end that forced the little animal to go into the person as the only possible exit from the device itself.

The practice later became known as "gerbiling" and was popular amongst the Hollywood elites in the 1970's, as well as by various royal families around the globe per long standing tradition to this day.

And though this sort of thing has occurred since Roman times, as depicted on their oil lamps, it wasn't until the patent of 1843 that the English perfected it and made it their own.

Today it is recognized as the official sport of the House of Lords.

In 2007 the team of Drs. Inisku and Gottschlang of the University of Offentitten in Nordsee proved that the molecular bonds in the brains of millennials were looser than the molecular bonds in the brains of previous generations. This was found to be the reason that no logical or sensible idea ever stays with millennials. Information simply falls between the cellular cracks, so to speak, producing what may well be regarded in the annals of history as the stupidest generation ever.

In a long running test conducted by the APSCA and ARRP with funding from The National Medicinal Institution, it was irrefutably established that, over a 20 year test span, randomly selected residents of Florida preferred the taste of synthetic cat food to either albacore or chicken.

Since early in it's statehood Texas had a law on the books outlawing "buggery perpetrated against livestock" but it was removed from the books in 1958 due to overwhelming public outcry after so many Texans were refused for the draft on the grounds of moral turpitude as a direct result of this law.

In 1964 the President issued pardons to all throughout the history of Texas who had been caught up under this law declaring that the Livestock Anti-Buggery Law had "affected every single family in Texas" was "contrary to Texas values" and had always been "stupid, fucked up, and shitty".

Today Texans make up the bulk of the US military.

In 1978 the State of Missouri won the honor of being the 12th safest third world country on the planet. It held that honor for the next 16 years before dropping to the 18th spot, where it currently resides well behind Belize but still ahead of Somalia.

The Canadian flag is a happy accident, as are most things Canadian. Originally a tanned sealskin decorated with beads and glass in the shape of the Union Jack and bearing the vague outline of a generic monarch, the flag was lost on the St. Lawrence river after a particularly nasty canoe accident. Subsequently a maple leaf was dipped in maple syrup and stuck to a pair of ladies drawers and then run up the flagpole over the nearby fort so it would be clear that the fort was still occupied. Due to budget reasons and a decline in the number of quality sealskin tanneries, the Canadian flag has forever since remained a maple leaf proud on a background of ladies drawers.
If you're ever lucky enough to be close to a new one you will be able to smell the maple scent that is infused in all Canadian flags since 1929 by royal decree.

Since the time of Napoleon all French government service hats have been lined with tinfoil out of "un exces de prudence".
This precedent was used to justify the mandatory use of tinfoil hat liners for all government service hats in the USA as prescribed by federal law since 2003 under redacted homeland security guidelines.

Benjamin Franklin was well known in the Continental Congress for his use of mercury suppositories to regulate body temperature based on the hypothesis that since mercury reacts to temperature then it must be able to absorb and regulate temperature as well.
This led to his famously documented discovery that was written up and later debated in the peer reviewed English Journal Of The Medicinal Arts determining that, "while fun, mercury suppositories are of absolutely no use whatsoever".

This verdict notwithstanding, the idea was revived in the 1980's by the US military in secret experiments using much larger (1L) mercury suppositories to lower the body temperature of GI's so as to render them invisible on thermal imaging.
The process reportedly remains in wide use, but details are classified.

It is well known that the media and educational system have been spreading lies and propaganda for decades. Despite that the public has learned through recent investigations, that in the same way that St Patrick rid Ireland of snakes, Abraham Lincoln freed America from vampires. Thank God for Abraham Lincoln!

While travelling through the American West in the mid 1800's
Oscar Wilde invented the Henri Oscillating Rifle.
When the rifle was set up and engaged it would fire in a sweeping back
and forth motion clearing anything in it's path until it finally ran out of
ammunition.
The device was later sold to the British Military who then
sold it to the Belgian Congo who in turn sold it
to the Rhodesians who promptly lost it.

In 1915 Pancho Villa with a band of followers raided the town of Columbus New Mexico in search of a clean outhouse.

Ambrose Bierce, writing for the Hearst papers, reported on the sorry state of Mexican outhouses, some "piled high with human waste and the carcasses of ghost chickens", saying that they were the "foulest and most vile aspect of this venture" that he had encountered.

Bierce later left in disgust and went south to Buenos Aires where he married into a local family of note and opened a dance hall.

The olympic games in ancient times were performed oiled up and in the nude, and ended with the winners publicly sodomizing the losers. That's why the olympic flag represents the sphincters of all races, equally.

Social Media was invented by the military with funding from the Five Eyes and the Bilderberg Group as a means of tracking the entire world population at all times. The working theory was that the bulk of humanity is so stupid that they will go willingly into this trap.

Child labor was deemed "good, proper, and necessary" by the US courts in the early 1900's on the basis that "childrens delicate hands are better suited for some things".
Interestingly, the Catholic Church had already come to the very same conclusion.

The State of Nevada has been designated as a UN World Site For The DIsposal Of Nuclear And Radioactive Waste. Beginning in 2050 all nuclear waste worldwide will be collected and deposited in central Nevada. On making the decision the US representative to the UN cast a yes vote. In later interviews she was asked about her yes vote and said, "Seriously? Why not? Have you seen Nevada?"

There is a secretive group in Rochester New York that has existed for over a hundred years called E Pluribus Enemus. They meet late at night once a month in randomly selected public parks for a ritualized group enema which they in turn spray onto the lawns.

Their mission statement since their inception has been that they are simply "performing a public service, fertilizing for the greater good, and making america green again.".

Canada has begun taking bids for a border wall just across the river from Buffalo New York. A New Zealand firm is in the lead to get the project which is slated to begin next year. After decades of study that included Canadian academics and politicians visiting Buffalo for repeated research missions one researcher summed it up by telling reporters, "We're gonna do it eh. I mean, you've been to Buffalo, right? We need to stop that disgusting filth from spreading north. Besides, a nice wall will block our view of the place. You've seen that mess over there eh?".

In 2005 the government made a secret deal with the auto makers so that when your little engine light goes on it sends a signal to an NSA computer that logs your location and turns on a recording device in the car for a 24 hour period.

This is part of the governments plan to track everyone all the time, much like the reason they invented social media.

It is also why they removed nearly all pay phones forcing everyone to buy a personal tracking device.

Chicago Butt Spiders (Arachnidae chicagoanusii) were first documented in the 1800's and were long thought to be an urban myth. However, the Smithsonian has a collection of seventeen Chicago Butt Spiders that were removed from Al Capones rectum when he was cavity searched after being transferred to the prison at Terminal Island. Endemic to Chicago, they are found no where else, and are particularly despised for their occassional infestations of the toilets at O'Hare Airport.

Science has proven that there are a finite number of cells in the body which means that when one body part is bigger then others must necessarily be smaller and correllating cell structures must be sacrificed. In Victorian times this was referred to in the medical profession as the "Inverse breast to brain ratio".

There was also noted a male correllation which came to be known colloquially as the "little dick syndrome" and was markedly increased worldwide amongst the political classes.

In 1967 Jeanette Fondaye published her guide to Hollywood studio beauty standards which gave the perfect head to body size ratio for all actors and actresses to be equal in dimensions to a lollipop.
It remains the standard to this day.

In 1979 a team at MIT working with a team from Oxford discovered that the human bowel was capable of creating the same conditions as the geologic forces used in the creation of diamonds and other precious gems.

The researchers found that refraining from excretion for a minimum of seven days would provide the exact pressure and heat to create gem stones.

They also found that by introducing various coloring agents into the food along with the required 300 grams of egg shells consumed daily by the subjects they could affect the final color of the gemstone.

For instance, consumption of only six bing cherries is required to create a stone with a deep kashmir ruby color, four maraschino cherries however produce a glowing pink, while several blue curacaos will produce a lovely dark sapphire. Clear flawless diamonds require no coloring agents and only a few days longer gestation to reach Mohs 10 hardness.

After a gestation of seven to sixteen days excretion is again resumed and the gemstones are carefully removed from the enveloping husks of waste.

The Diamond Cartel has long sought to suppress the results of this study for fear that their artificially inlated product pricing will suffer a setback toward a pricing model that more reflects reality, considering that diamonds are apparently as common as turds.

The English have always been known to take the things they love with them wherever they go. In colonial India they developed a type of inexpensive ale that was overall a decent ale with the one unwelcome side effect of causing the most violent intestinal disruptions, likely a result of using polluted water and spoiled hops.

As a result this ale was dubbed Intestinal Parasite Ale, or I.P.A. for short. Later when this style of ale was brewed in London under slightly more sterile circumstances it no longer caused the unpleasant intestinal reactions with such great regularity and the name was quietly changed to India Pale Ale, still keeping the I.P.A. moniker as a nod to it's colonial-dysynteric origins.

It is still very popular in England to suggest that the name was really changed for marketing purposes in export to America because "American sensibilities are so much more simple, puritanical, and prudish", with many going so far as to dismiss the Americans simply as "fannies".

Shortly after German reunification in 1989 the newly unified federal government decreed that prostitution would be legal and regulated, and that prostitutes could either be paid in deutschmarks, euros, or the traditional payment for German prostitutes, turnips.

The standard payment for a three hour sex romp was deemed to be a minimum of 9 medium sized turnips per prostitute involved, with an extra turnip each for the madam and/or pimp.

Needless to say, during the 1990's, in Germany and particularly the former East Germany, turnips were often sold out or otherwise in short supply. This was rectified by an act of parliament heavily subsidizing turnip farms, and a ratification of higher import quotas of turnips from neighboring Holland. In 2016 German demands for English turnips were seen as contributing to the English voting decisively to leave the EU which the EU later acknowledged should have hardly been surprising "knowing how much the English value a well built turnip".

According to Kern County officials in California the letter grades used to designate restaurant cleanliness in Los Angeles County have a historical attachment to institutionalized racism. **A** was the letter grade given to white owned restaurants with the inherent assumption that they had recieved the top grade and were correspondingly clean. **B** was the letter grade given to "bean joints" and implied the presence of vermin, feces, or otherwise unsanitary conditions. **C** was the grade given to Chinese restaurants ostensibly because they slow cooked their beef and pork never reaching food safety temperatures. Unfortunately some of the older inspectors continue to retain their racist outlooks.

The next time you are in Los Angeles take a look at the letter grades in restaurant windows and realize that the subtle practice of institutionalized racism in L. A. restaurant letter grades continues to this day.

It is well known that in China rhinoceros horn is consumed as a magical health elixer said to give the user "boner for days". It is also well known that rhinoceros horn and human hair are both composed of keratin. What is not so widely known are the workings of the underground market in China for human pubic hair which is harvested by the government, pressed into faux rhino horn, sold by the kilo, and consumed in the same way as authentic rhino horn. All across China the unsuspecting tourist as well as the native citizen are being served pubic hair mixed with viagra in lieu of rhino horn, still giving the end user that familiar keratin flavor and "boner for days", while easing the poaching pressure on rhinos world wide.

A long running survey of members of the U.S. House of Representatives found that on average over the course of the 20th century more than 99% but slightly less than 100% of House members had been repeatedly abused as a child, and had learned to believe that it was normal and ok behaviour, which in turn directly fueled their desire for a career in politics.

In 1921 doctors in Winnipeg and Ottowa published a paper in the Canadian Medicinal Reviewer stating that Canadian girls were being born with everted vaginas. This phenomonon had been documented across the country, they said, and it was baffling medical professionals across Canada.

When doctors from the United States and Europe reviewed the evidence they pointed out that those were not girls with everted vaginas but instead were little boys with penises.

The authors of the original study responded to press inquiries saying "Ah, that makes sense eh."

In an address to the US Senate Comittee on Bookbinding and Publication Mr. Yuseph Blattstein of the Publishers Circle Guild complained that American authors "cannot make a living, at all, due to the fact that every single word has been copyrighted by the Merriam Webster Company". He went on to suggest that if it weren't for Hollywood and the film industry turning those words into pictures then American authors would not make any money at all and would have to stop writing stories completely. Republican Senator Chiam Berger promised to look into the situation saying "it is a travesty that words can be owned and pictures are still free." When asked about poetry and childrens books the Senator waved his hand dismissively and laughed and walked away.

In 1973 Los Angeles California was in the midst of a threefold crisis involving a shortage of petroleum fuels, ongoing drought with rising air temperatures, and severe air pollution. While various government agencies and university-led research groups worked on possible solutions to these problems, only one offered a possible fast remedy and that was in regard to the severe air pollution. It was discovered by a research group from Cal State that individuals could reduce nearly 80% of measurable air pollution simply by "breathing" through their anus. This was described in the literature (and reported on by the Herald 7-21-73) as "a sort of kegel-type exercise where one repeatedly draws air into their anus, holds it for a ten count, and then releases it again". This was repeated often throughout the day. By doing so the toxins in the air were removed to the mucous membranes of the anus and then excreted, thus removing pollutants directly from the air. Within two years the air quality of Los Angeles had improved greatly, and has continued to do so ever since thanks to ordinance 2FU-1897226.563 passed in L.A. County in 1994 mandating that "all Angelenos must perform this exercise daily and frequently" as a public service.

China is currently looking into implementing this practice across all of its manufacturing centers with compulsory pilot projects ordered by the central governmnet starting in Beijing spring of 2025.

In 1899 the automobile alternator was invented by an Amish farmer in the small Pennsylvania town of Bird-In-Hand. Jakob Schmidt and his son Irv Schmidt built the first alternator out of wooden parts held together by mortise and tenon pins with all moving parts greased with hog lard and the coil wrapped with copper wire from chicken cooping. The finished alternator was activated by the movement of the axle on Jakobs buggy and served to play a lively tune on a tiny wooden set of pipes and bellows announcing his arrival at nearby farms with a variety of home made pastries and ice cream treats in his buggy.

While few people remember that Jakob Schmidt invented the alternator, even fewer realize that it was only invented in the service of Jakobs other popular invention, the ice cream buggy.

Afterword

I have been informed by my editors that in consideration of the demographic that this book is written for I should, for obvious reasons, keep this book short. My page editor has even suggested it is already too long and shouldn't take any longer to read than the time it takes the average American to drop a duece.

I however, disagree. I believe in you, I have faith in your ability to read a full thirty to forty pages of one and a half spaced set typeface that doesn't ever even fill the page, I believe in you.

So, knowing that you have enough of that can-do spirit to read at least thirty but not quite forty pages of words, I will accede to my editors demands and stop here, but rest assured that at this very moment I have just begun True Stories, Volume 2 so that you can continue your journey of growth and knowledge and exploration into the complex, muddled, and multi-layered world of facts.

D. Saige Elldurs
2020

About the Author:
D. Saige Elldurs, is an award winning philosoph, historian, and leading forensic bird call specialist.

This book is satire and is a work of purest fiction.
Any resemblance of characters and entities depicted in this book to persons or entities living or dead, past or present, is purely coincidental and is in no way rooted in our shared reality.
Same goes for corporations, governments, religions, etc.

Lightning Source UK Ltd.
Milton Keynes UK
UKHW051255220820
368606UK00027B/697